Super Safari

1

Letters and Numbers Workbook

CAMBRIDGE
UNIVERSITY PRESS

Colour in Polly!

CAMBRIDGE
UNIVERSITY PRESS

University Printing House, Cambridge CB2 8BS, United Kingdom

One Liberty Plaza, 20th Floor, New York, NY 10006, USA

477 Williamstown Road, Port Melbourne, VIC 3207, Australia

314–321, 3rd Floor, Plot 3, Splendor Forum, Jasola District Centre, New Delhi – 110025, India

103 Penang Road, #05-06/07, Visioncrest Commercial, Singapore 238467

Cambridge University Press is part of the University of Cambridge.

It furthers the University's mission by disseminating knowledge in the pursuit of education, learning and research at the highest international levels of excellence.

www.cambridge.org
Information on this title: www.cambridge.org/9781316628164

First published 2016

20 19 18 17 16 15

Printed in Great Britain by CPI Group (UK) Ltd, Croydon CR0 4YY

A catalogue record for this publication is available from the British Library

ISBN 978-1-316-62816-4 Paperback

Additional resources for this publication at www.cambridge.org/supersafari

Super Safari 1
Letters and Numbers Workbook

Hello!

The children trace the circle with their index finger. Then they trace the circle with different coloured crayons several times. Finally, the children colour the picture freely.

1 Trace and colour.

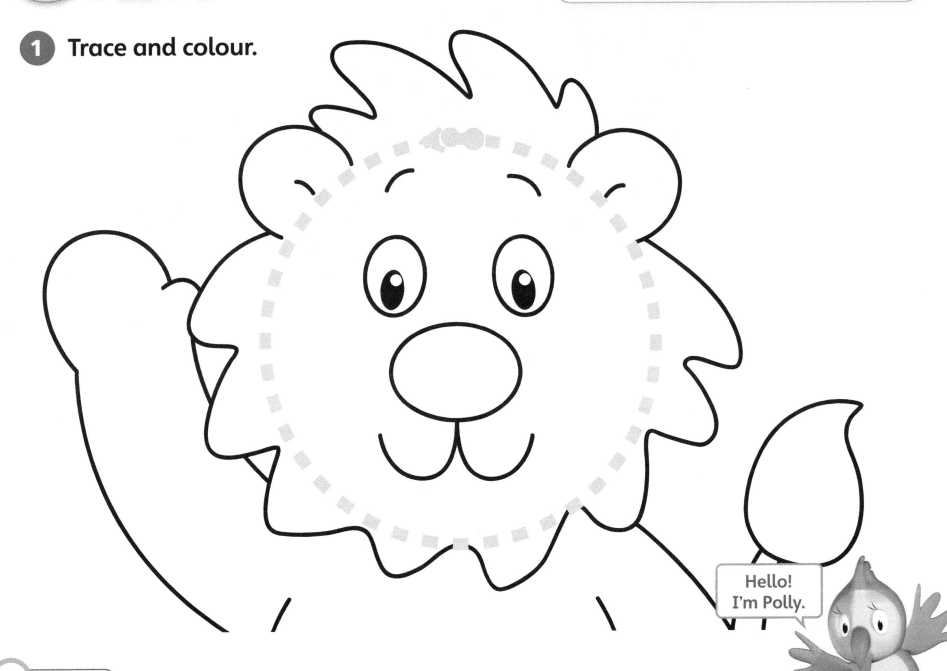

Hello! I'm Polly.

1 **Colour the pictures.**

The children point to the girl in the picture and say *hello* aloud. Repeat the procedure with the boy. Finally, the children colour the picture freely.

1 My class

The children trace the lines with their index finger first, and then with different coloured crayons several times. Then they identify the objects. Finally, the children colour the pictures freely.

1 Trace and colour.

1 **Count and trace. Colour the objects.**

1   2

1 **Trace and colour.**

1 **Count and trace. Colour the pictures.**

1 **Trace and colour.**

The children trace the lines with their index finger first, and then with different coloured crayons. The children identify the book, the boy, the girl and the school. The children point to the pictures. Finally, the children colour the pictures freely.

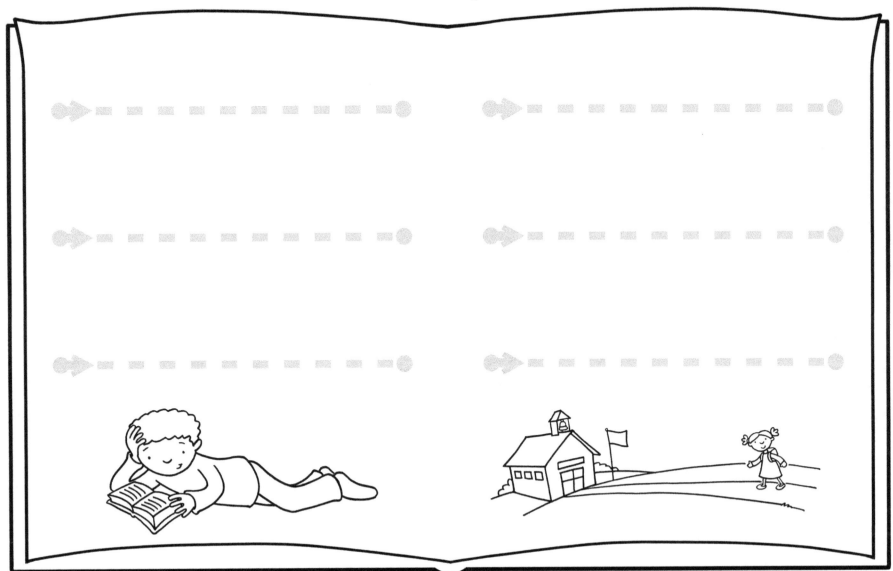

1 **Count and colour. Trace the numbers.**

The children point to the characters and count them aloud. Then the children colour them. Finally, they trace the numbers with different coloured crayons several times.

1 Trace and colour.

The children say /p/ – /p/ – /p/ – *pencil*. Then they trace the letter and colour in the picture freely. Finally, the children colour the pictures that start with the sound /p/.

1 Colour and cut. Assemble the booklet.

Fold

Fold

Colour and cut. Assemble the booklet.

Materials:

scissors, crayons

Instructions:

The children name the items. Then they colour in the objects. Help children cut out the booklet. Finally, help the children fold the pages to make the booklet.

1 **Match and colour.**

 Ask the children to point to the different objects. Then the children match the objects with the corresponding grey shadow. Finally, the children colour the objects freely.

2 My colours

The children trace the lines with their index finger and with different coloured crayons several times. Then the children identify the objects and colour them freely.

1 Trace and colour.

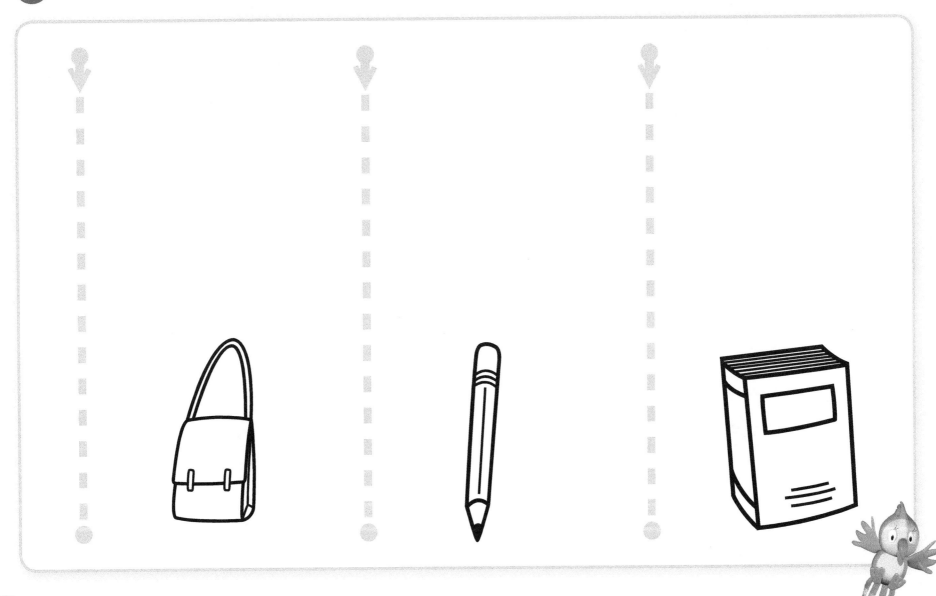

1 **Count and trace. Colour the objects.**

The children count the cans aloud. Then they trace the number with their index finger first, and then with different coloured crayons several times. Finally, the children colour the cans of paint according to the instructions: *Point to the can. Colour the can red.*

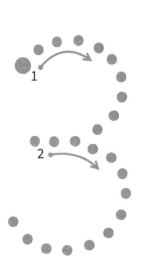

1 Trace and colour.

The children trace the lines with their index finger, and then with different coloured crayons several times. Finally, the children colour the crayons freely.

1 Count and trace. Colour the objects.

The children count the books aloud. Then the children trace the number with their index finger first, and then with different coloured crayons several times. Finally, the children colour the picture freely.

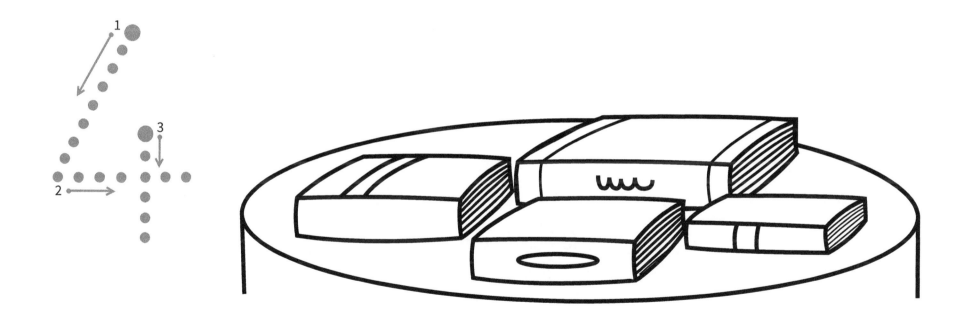

1 Trace and colour.

The children trace the lines with different coloured crayons.
Finally, the children name and colour the characters freely.

1 **Count and trace. Colour the pictures.**

The children count the girls aloud. Then they trace the numbers with different coloured crayons several times. Finally, they colour the pictures freely.

1 **Trace and colour.**

The children say /b/ – /b/ – /b/ – *bag*. Then they trace the letter and colour in the picture freely. Finally, the children colour the pictures that start with the sound /b/.

1 Colour and glue.

Colour and glue.

Materials:
scissors, coloured tissue paper (blue, green, yellow), glue, coloured markers

Preparation:
Cut small squares of coloured tissue paper.

Instructions:
The children use a blue marker to colour in the first section in the rainbow. Then distribute glue and the blue tissue paper. Help the children spread the glue on the blue section. Show the children how to glue the blue tissue paper on the corresponding section. Continue in the same manner with the green and yellow sections of the rainbow.

1 **Trace and colour the objects.**

The children trace the objects. Then they colour in the objects freely.

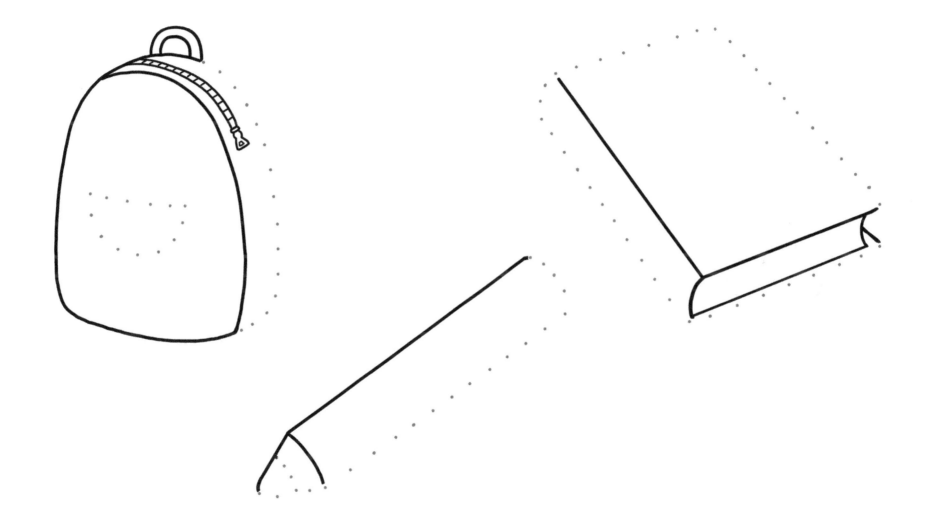

3 My family

The children trace the circle with their index finger first, and then with different coloured crayons several times. Finally, the children identify the family members and colour the picture freely.

1 Trace and colour.

1 **Count and trace. Colour the pictures.**

The children identify the family members and count them aloud. Then they trace the numbers with different coloured crayons several times. Finally, the children colour the pictures freely.

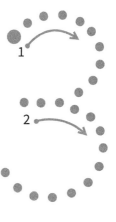

1 Trace and colour.

The children trace the circles with different coloured crayons several times. Finally, the children identify the family member and colour the picture freely.

1 **Count and match.**

The children identify and count the members of each family. Then they match the family to the corresponding number. Finally, they colour the pictures.

1 2 3 4

1 Trace and colour.

The children trace the circles with different coloured crayons several times.
Finally, the children identify the family members and colour the pictures freely.

1 **Trace and count. Colour the pictures.**

The children identify and trace the numbers. Then they identify the family members. Finally, they colour the corresponding number of people.

1 **Trace and colour.**

The children say /d/ – /d/ – /d/ – *dad*. Then they trace the letter and colour in the picture freely. Finally, the children colour the pictures that start with the sound /d/.

1 Colour and assemble the puzzle.

Colour and assemble the puzzle.

Materials:
crayons, scissors, glue, paper (1 sheet per student)

Instructions:
The children identify the family members.
Then the children colour the picture.
Help them cut out the puzzle pieces.
The children assemble the puzzle and
glue it onto a sheet of paper.

1 **Draw your family.**

The children draw their families inside the picture frame.
Finally, they describe their families to the rest of the class.

This is my family.

4 My toys

The children trace the lines with their index fingers first, and then with different coloured crayons. Finally, the children identify the toys and colour them in freely.

1 Trace and colour.

1 **Count and trace. Colour the picture.**

The children count the balls aloud. Then the children trace the number with their index finger first, and then with different coloured crayons several times. Finally, the children colour the picture.

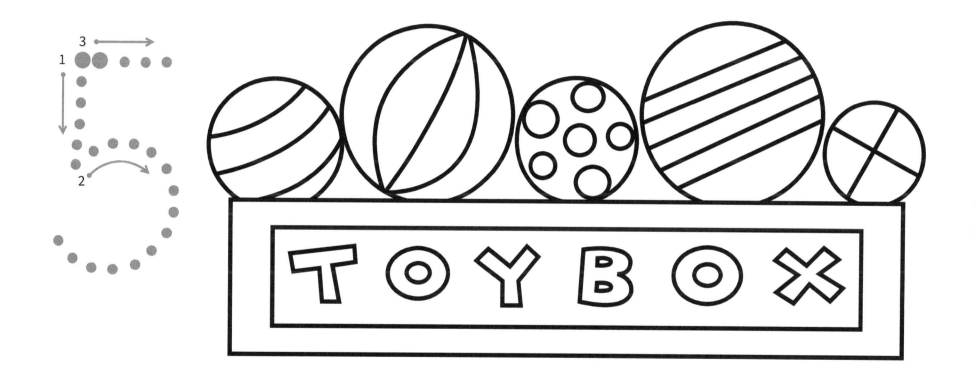

1 Trace and say.

The children trace the lines with their index finger first, and then with different coloured crayons. Finally, the children say the patterns: *big ball, small ball, big ball, small ball; big doll, small doll …*

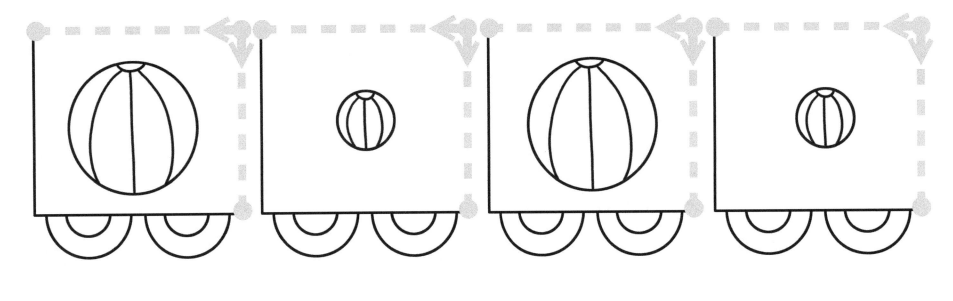

1 **Count and trace. Colour the picture.**

The children count the dolls aloud. Then the children trace the number with their index finger first, and then with different coloured crayons several times. Finally, the children colour the picture freely.

1 **Trace and colour.**

The children trace all the lines with different coloured crayons. Then the children name the character and the toys. Finally, the children colour in the picture.

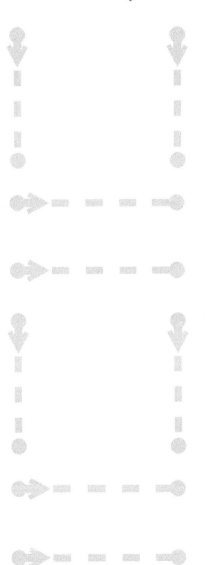

1 **Count and colour.**

The children identify the numbers. Then they count the toys aloud. Finally, the children colour the pictures freely.

1 2 3 4 5 6

1 **Trace and colour.**

The children say /k/ – /k/ – /k/ – *car*. Then the children trace the letter and colour in the picture freely. Finally, the children colour the pictures that start with the sound /k/.

1 Colour and cut. Play a game.

Colour and cut. Play a game.

Materials:

crayons, scissors

Instructions:

The children colour the cards. Help them cut the cards out.

Demonstrate how the *Memory game* is played.

Divide the class into pairs. Each pair uses only one set of cards. They shuffle the cards and place them face down on the table. Then each child takes a turn turning over two cards and finding matching pairs. The child with the most pairs of cards wins.

1 **Cut and glue.**

The children colour in the toy box with coloured crayons. Then the children look for pictures of toys in old magazines. Help the children cut out the pictures. Finally, the children glue the pictures inside the toy box.

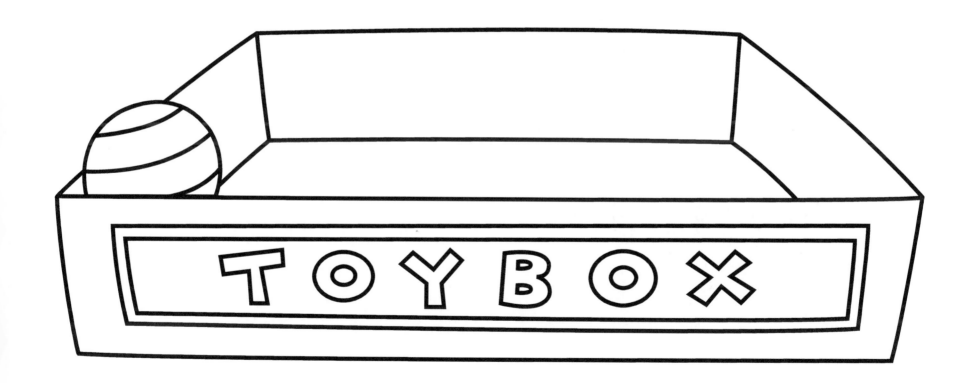

5 My numbers

The children trace the lines with their index finger first, and then they trace the circles with different coloured crayons several times. Finally, the children colour the picture freely.

1 Trace and colour.

1 **Trace and draw.**

The children identify and trace the numbers with different colours. Then they draw the corresponding number of objects, e.g. *one book, two crayons, three balls.*

1   1   1

2   2   2

3   3   3

1 **Trace and colour.**

The children trace the circles with their index finger first, and then they trace them with different coloured crayons. Finally, the children colour the picture freely.

1 **Trace. Count and colour.**

The children say the numbers aloud. Then they trace the numbers with different coloured crayons. Finally, the children count and colour the corresponding number of items.

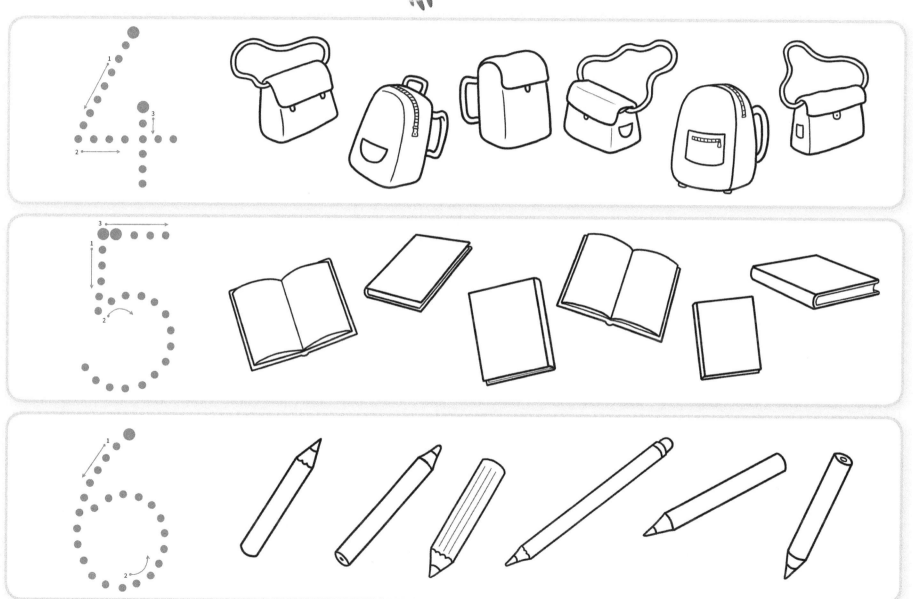

1 **Trace and say.**

The children trace the circles with their index finger first, and then they trace the circles with different coloured crayons. Finally, the children identify the items.

1 **Count and match.**

The children identify the numbers. Then they count and match the numbers with the corresponding items. Finally, they colour the items freely.

1 2 3 4 5

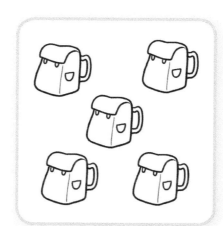

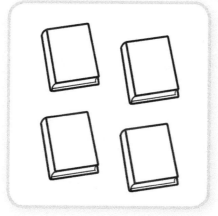

1 Trace and colour.

The children say /t/ – /t/ – /t/ – *teddy*. Then the children trace the letter and colour in the picture freely. Finally, the children colour the pictures that start with the sound /t/.

1 Cut and assemble. Spin and say.

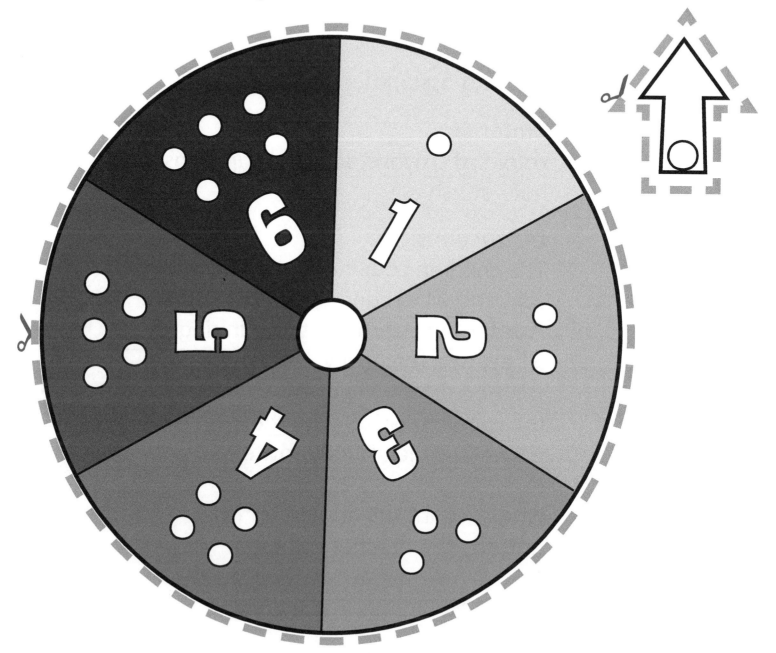

Cut and assemble. Spin and say.

Materials:
coloured crayons, scissors, paper fastener, hole punch

Instructions:
The children colour and cut out the spinning wheel and the arrow. Punch a hole through the spinning wheel and the arrow. Help the children attach the arrow to the spinning wheel with the paper fastener. Finally, invite different children to spin their wheel, count the number of dots and say the number out loud.

1 **Draw and count.**

The children draw one more toy in each box. The children count aloud the total number of toys in each toy box. Finally, the children colour in the pictures freely.

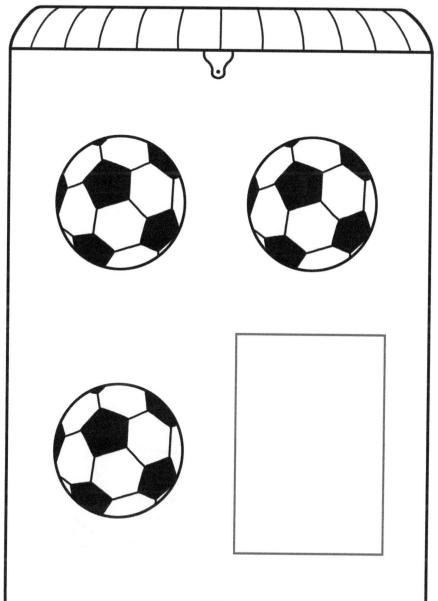

The children trace the spiral with their index finger first, and then they trace it with different coloured crayons three times. Finally, the children identify the pet and colour the picture freely.

1 Trace and colour.

1 **Trace and count. Colour the picture.**

The children trace the number with their index finger first, and then with different coloured crayons several times. Finally, they count the cats aloud and colour the picture freely.

1

2

1 Trace and colour.

The children trace the spirals with different coloured crayons. Then they identify the pets and name them aloud. Finally, they colour in the picture freely.

My letters

1 **Count and trace. Colour the picture.**

The children count the birds aloud. Then they trace the number with their index finger first, and then with different coloured crayons several times. Finally, the children colour in the picture freely.

1 **Trace and say. Colour the pictures.**

The children trace the spirals with different coloured crayons. Then they identity the actions and the pets. Finally, the children colour the pets freely.

1 Count and circle.

The children count the pets aloud. Then the children circle the corresponding numbers. Finally, the children colour the pets freely.

7 / 8

7 / 8

1 **Trace and colour.**

1 Cut and assemble.

Cut and assemble.

Materials:
construction paper, scissors, crayons, glue stick

Instructions:
The children colour in the bird and the clouds. Then help the children cut out the pictures. Next, help them glue the bird and the clouds onto construction paper and cut them out again. Show the children how to assemble the bird to make it stand.

1 Match and colour.

The children point to the pets: *Point to the small bunny.* *Point to the big bunny.* The children match the big pets to the small pets. Finally, the children colour the pets.

7 My food

1 **Trace and colour.**

1 **Count and trace.**

The children count the scoops of ice cream aloud. Then the children trace the numbers with different coloured crayons. Finally, they colour in the pictures freely.

1 **Trace and colour.**

The children trace the "s" shape with their index finger first, and then with different coloured crayons several times. Finally, the children identify the food and colour the pictures freely.

1 **Count and circle. Colour the pictures.**

The children count the vegetables aloud, and then they circle the corresponding number. Finally, the children colour the pictures freely.

5/6

7/8

1 **Trace and say. Colour the pictures.**

The children trace the "s" shapes with different coloured crayons. The children identify the food and say whether they like it or not: *Laura, what is this? Spaghetti. I like spaghetti.* Finally, the children colour the food freely.

1 **Count and match. Trace the numbers.**

The children count the number of slices in each cake aloud. Then they match the cakes with the corresponding numbers. Finally, the children trace the numbers.

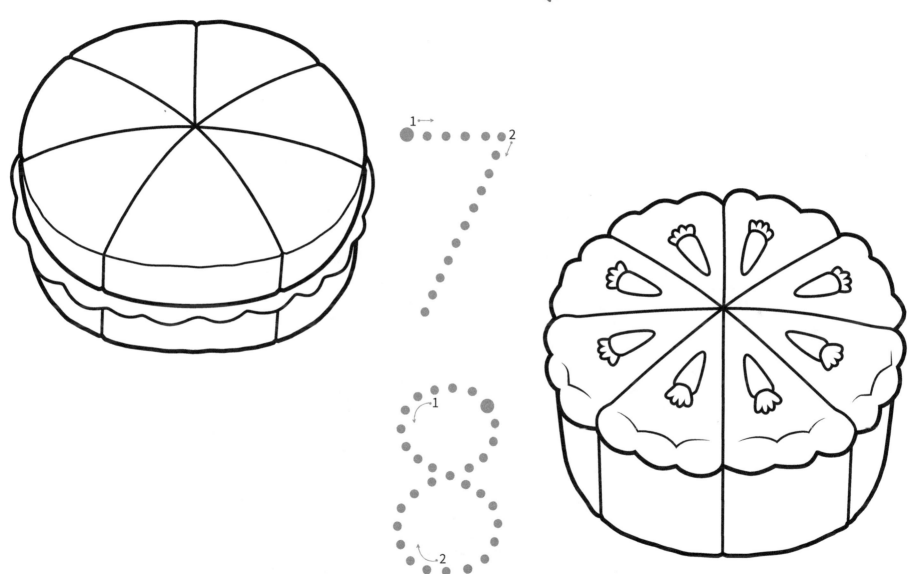

1 Trace and colour.

The children say /s/ – /s/ – /s/ – *salad*. Then they trace the letter and colour in the picture freely. Finally, the children colour the pictures that start with the sound /s/.

1 Colour and glue.

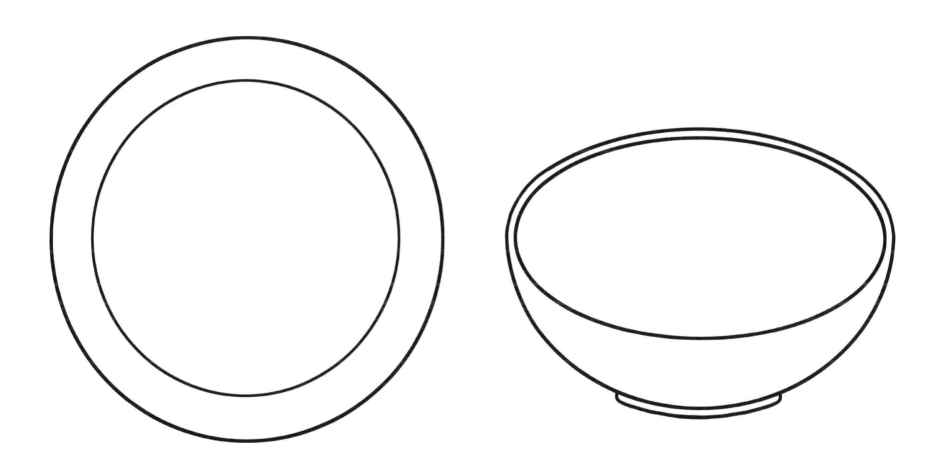

Colour and glue.

Materials:
coloured markers, yellow wool, rice,
glue, scissors

Preparation:
Cut the wool into 10-cm lengths.

Instructions:
The children colour in the plate and the bowl
with the markers. Then they glue
the yellow wool onto the plate as
spaghetti. Next, the children spread
glue inside the bowl and sprinkle on
some rice. Finally, the children say
if they like the food or not.

1 **Match and say. Colour the pictures.**

The children point to the food. Then they match the food they like to the happy face. Next, the children say *I like* … . Finally, the children colour in the pictures.

The children trace the lines with their index finger first, and then with different coloured crayons several times. Finally, the children identify each of the clothing items and colour the pictures freely.

1 Trace and colour.

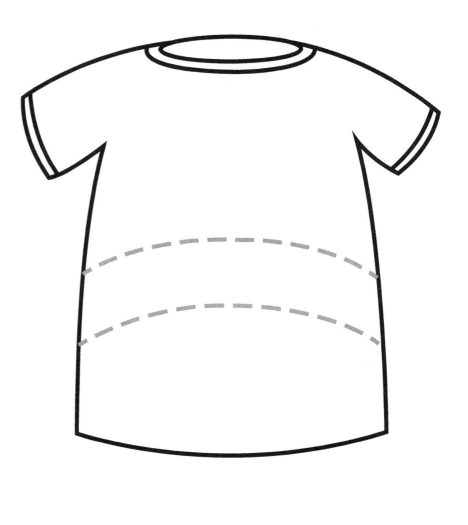

1 **Count and trace. Colour the picture.**

The children count the T-shirts aloud. Then the children trace the number with their index finger first, and then with different coloured crayons several times. Finally, the children colour in the picture.

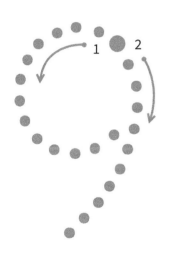

1 **Trace and say. Colour the pictures.**

1 **Count and trace. Colour the picture.**

The children count the shoes aloud. Then the children trace the number with their index finger first, and then with different coloured crayons several times. Finally, they colour in the picture.

1 **Trace. Listen and colour.**

The children trace the lines with different coloured crayons. Then the children follow instructions to colour in the clothing items: *Show me your blue crayon. Colour the T-shirt blue.*

1 **Count and colour. Trace the numbers.**

The children count the clothing items aloud. Then they colour them in. Finally, the children trace the numbers with different coloured crayons.

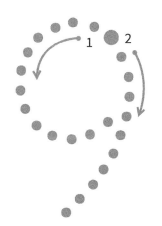

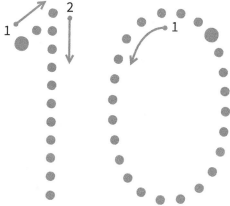

1 **Trace and colour.**

The children say /n/ – /n/ – /n/ – *net*. Then they trace the letter and colour in the picture freely. Finally, the children colour the pictures that start with the sound /n/.

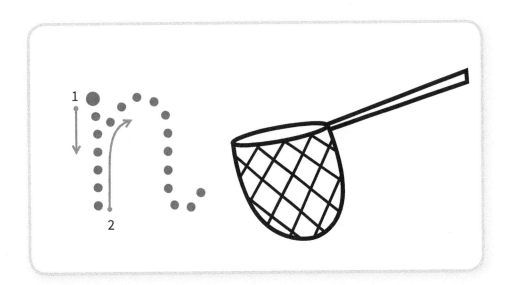

1 Make a clothes line.

Fold

Fold

Fold

Fold

Make a clothes line.

Materials:
coloured crayons, string, scissors

Preparation:
Cut out string the length of your classroom.
Hang it to make a clothes line inside the
classroom at children's eye level.

Instructions:
The children colour in the clothes. Then they
cut out the pieces. Help the children fold
the flaps on the clothing items.
Finally, the children hang their
clothes on the clothes line.

1 **Listen and colour. Match the clothes.**

Give the children instructions to colour the clothing items in the boxes: *Colour the T-shirt blue.* Then the children match the clothing items in the boxes to the boy's clothes.

The children trace the shapes with different coloured crayons. Then the children identify the playground equipment. Finally, the children colour in the pictures freely.

1 Trace and colour.

   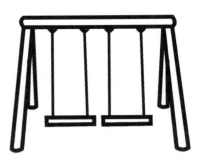

1 **Count and trace.**

The children count the characters aloud and trace the numbers with different coloured crayons. Finally, they colour the pictures freely.

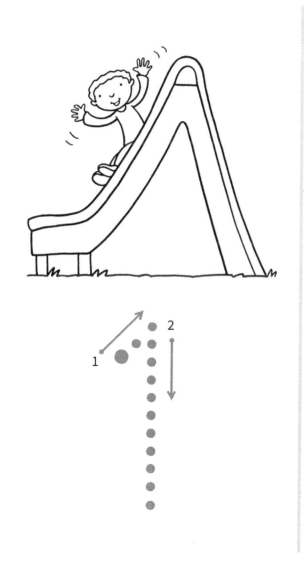

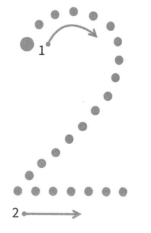

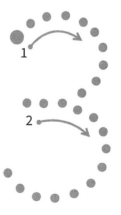

1 Trace and colour.

The children trace the shapes with different coloured crayons. Say sentences and have children identify the pictures: *Point to the boy. Down you go! Point to the girl. Up you go!* Finally, the children colour them freely.

1 Count and trace. Colour the picture.

The children count the characters in the picture. Then they trace the numbers with different coloured crayons. Finally, the children colour the pictures freely.

1 **Trace and colour.**

The children trace over the shapes with different coloured crayons. They name the playground equipment. Finally, the children colour in the scene.

n u n u n u n u

o i o i o i o i

1 **Count and trace.**

The children count each of the shapes aloud. Then they trace the numbers with different coloured crayons.

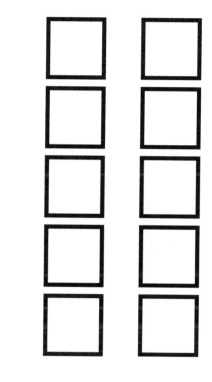

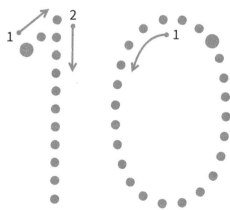

1 **Trace and colour.**

The children say /ɪ/ – /ɪ/ – /ɪ/ – *igloo*. Then the children trace the letter and colour in the picture freely. Finally, they colour the pictures that start with the sound /ɪ/.

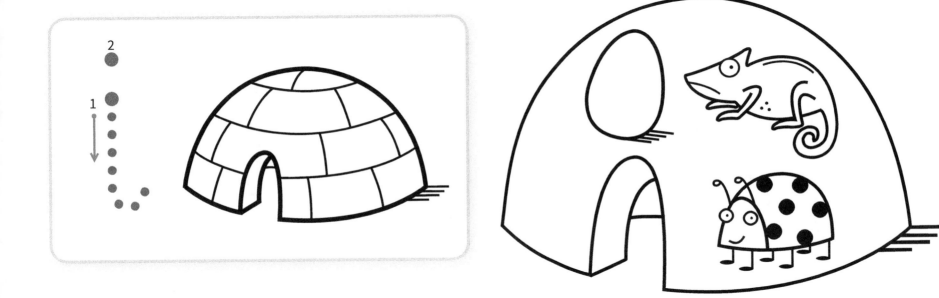

1 Make a park.

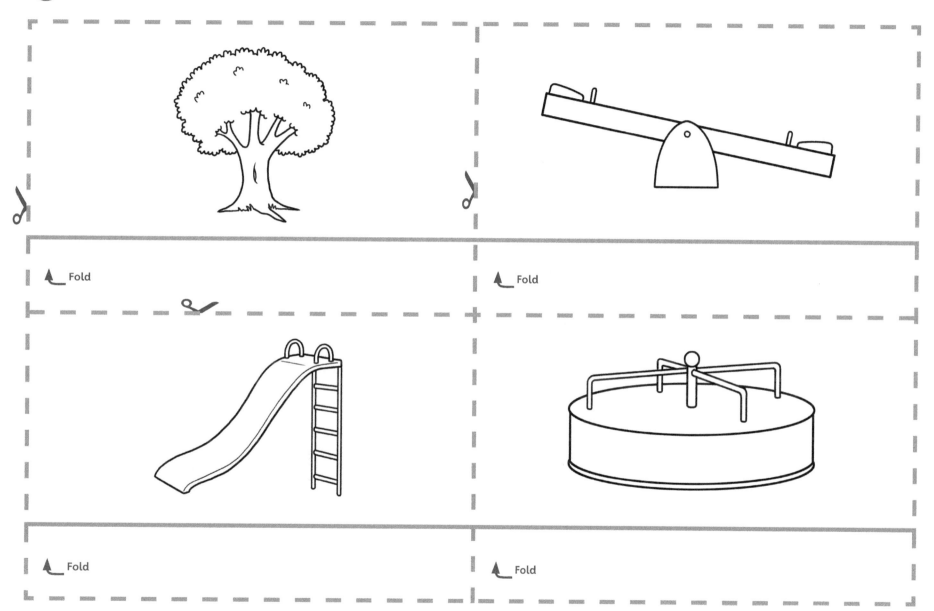

Fold

Fold

Fold

Fold

Make a park.

Materials:
scissors, glue, crayons, shoebox lid, green markers

Instructions:
The children colour in the pictures and cut them out. Then they identify the playground equipment and the tree. Next, the children colour the shoebox lid green. Show the children how to fold the bottom of each of the pictures to make them stand, and glue them onto the lid.

1 Look and match.

The children identify the big and small playground equipment. Then give instructions for children to match the big playground equipment with the small one. Finally, the children colour the pictures freely.

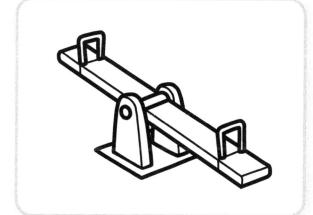

Thanks and acknowledgements

The publishers are grateful to the following contributors:

Blooberry Design: cover design, book design, publishing management and page make-up
Bill Bolton: cover illustration

The publishers and authors are grateful to the following illustrators:

Bill Bolton 1, 4, 20, 23, 40, 43, 46, 69, 90, (1 and repeats on all pages of Polly); Louise Gardner 6, 7, 8, 11, 15, 18, 25, 28, 30, 35, 38, 41, 49, 51, 55, 59, 60, 68, 73, 75, 77, 80, 85; Marek Jagucki 31, 43, 53, 58, 63, 67, 71, 81, 83, 95; Sue King (Plum Pudding) 5, 10, 21, 27, 61, 65, 78, 79, 87, 88, 89, 93; Bernice Lum 9, 12, 13, 16, 17, 19, 22, 26, 29, 32, 33, 36, 37, 39, 42, 45, 48, 50, 52, 56, 57, 62, 66, 70, 72, 76, 82, 86, 92